LIVING IN A STONE AGE SETTLEMENT

By Robin Twiddy

LIFE
LONG AGO

BookLife
PUBLISHING

©This edition is published in
2022. First published in 2019.
BookLife Publishing Ltd.
King's Lynn
Norfolk, PE30 4LS, UK

ISBN: 978-1-78637-548-3

Written by:
Robin Twiddy

Edited by:
Emilie Dufresne

Designed by:
Danielle Jones

IMAGE CREDITS

Cover & throughout - Anna Panova, Roxiller13, Vasif Maharov, Vialas, Oceloti, Radiocat. 4 - DenisKrivoy. 5 - popular business,
Lucy Ya, GoodStudio. 7 - Macrovector, Julia Dolzhenko. 8 - Dmitriy Nikiforov. 9 - Maquiladora. 10 - Midorie. 11 - armi1961.
12 - JC_Silver, Val_Iva. 13 - perori. 14 - Anton Malina. 15 - FcnixSPB, Andrii Bezvershenko. 17 - Rimma Z, Piotr Przyluski.
18 - Dimassbp - Hart PS94. 20 - Darla Hallmark. 22 - Art Alex, Vanatchanan, Top Vector Studio, Francois Poirier. 23 - PILart.
Images are courtesy of Shutterstock.com. With thanks to Getty Images, Thinkstock Photo and iStockphoto.

CONTENTS

Words that look like THIS can be found in the glossary on page 24.

A HOME of STONE

Hi, my name is Aliath and this is my home. Our people used to be <u>NOMADS</u> – this meant they travelled around and didn't have a <u>PERMANENT</u> home. But now we live in this settlement all the time with our friends and family.

People call this time the Neolithic (say: nee-oh-lith-ik) period - but that just means the 'New Stone Age'.

Most of our homes are just one big room with a hearth in the middle. A hearth is a fireplace. We use this to keep us warm and to cook. Look, you can see our stone beds and stone shelves. I keep my animal furs and skins there.

Here in the Stone Age, we weave materials to make fabric. We use this fabric to make our clothes.

STONE AGE CHORES

My mum and dad are farmers. We don't have schools so I spend my days working with my parents. Today I need to <u>TRADE</u> with some of the villagers, help Dad in the fields, gather some food for supper and go to the stone circle.

It's always busy in the village; everyone has jobs to do, even the children.

Oh, look over there! Our neighbours are building a new house. Can you see these bricks? They are made from mud! Mud is a really handy building material because it is everywhere. We squish the mud into brick shapes, then dry them by the fire.

Builders use stone as well. The roof will be made from a dried grass such as straw.

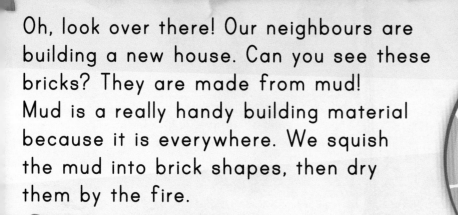

TRADING

Before we settled down, all we did was hunt and gather food. Now we can make and build all sorts of things. Let's go and see what we can trade. Dad has given me some barley to trade for tools.

ARROWHEADS AND SPEARS

These are used for protecting the settlement and hunting.

SCRAPER

These are used to <u>BUTCHER</u> animals and remove their meat.

POLISHED STONE AXE

These are used as weapons and for chopping down trees to make room for farming.

The knapper is the person that makes sharp stone tools by knocking stones together and then polishing them. He's got some great tools to trade today.

The HUNTERS

I saw Akatet and some others from the village heading into the woods with bows, arrows and spears. They must have gone hunting. We have lots of food from farming but some of the villagers still hunt for meat.

Oh look, there's Karnath, he must be late for the hunt.

When they return, we will have meat to eat and animal <u>HIDES</u> for the tanner. The tanner takes the animal hides and turns them into leather. This is then used to make clothes for us to wear.

This is an animal hide being stretched and dried.

JEWELLERY and ART

When we were travelling hunter-gatherers, we didn't have much time to learn how to make nice or useful things. Now that we have plenty of food, and a safe place to live, we have the time to figure out lots of new skills.

Look at this art that Sharbeth has painted onto the side of her house.

We also make jewellery and small statues. I traded some wheat for this bracelet and my friend Durff showed me how to make this. It's a <u>FERTILITY</u> goddess. I made it with this great stuff we discovered called clay. It starts wet, but if you leave it near the fire, it turns really hard!

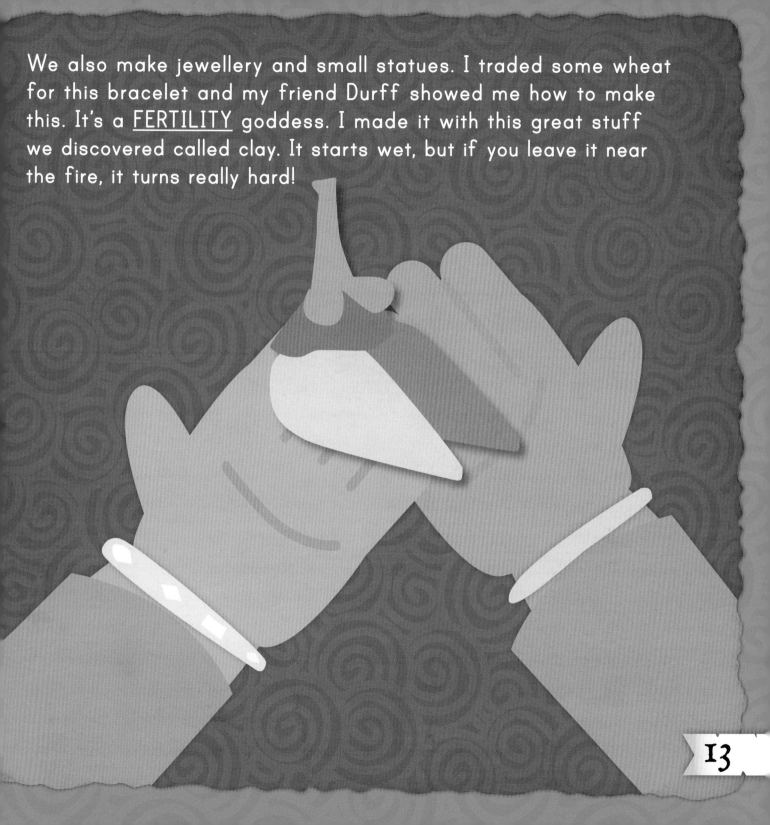

FARMING

Here is my Dad's field. He grows wheat and barley. Since we settled in one place, our new TECHNOLOGIES have made farming a lot easier. Apparently, we didn't really have enough food to trade until we settled!

Now we have a SURPLUS of food, meaning people are living longer and our community is growing bigger!

To help our plants grow big and strong, we dig ditches and grooves into the land. This means that when it rains a lot, the water just runs away from the <u>CROPS</u> and they don't get flooded.

Growing food is much better than gathering it. Why didn't we do this before?

ANIMALS

We used to hunt animals, but now we keep some on our land as well. These are called <u>DOMESTICATED</u> animals. We keep sheep, goats, cows and pigs. Having domesticated animals means that we have meat and milk whenever we need it. My favourite is goat's milk!

This is Ruff, our dog. He helps Mum and Dad <u>HERD</u> the animals. He also helps protect the village. If other humans or wild animals threaten our village, Ruff and his friends make lots of noise to let us know there is trouble.

Good boy, Ruff!

BUILDING a TEMPLE

Look over there! We are building a new TEMPLE. This will be a really great place for us all to get together. This is going to be the biggest and most impressive building in the village!

The whole village will come here for important CEREMONIES.

Let's take a closer look. Hey, is that limestone? That is much fancier than the mud bricks we use to build our homes. They also said that the walls will be covered with plaster and then painted.

I wonder how the builders got those heavy stones up there?

19

The STONE CIRCLE

It's a great place to meet new friends.

Oh! It's getting dark. We are all supposed to meet at the stone circle tonight. It is a little way outside of the village. We share it with all the other local villages and meet there for ceremonies and parties!

I bet this place will seem really <u>MYSTERIOUS</u> to people in the future!

The stone circle has lots of different uses; some of them are religious, some are social and some of the villagers can use it to read the stars. The stone circle has been here longer than I've been alive. I think that all the local clans helped build it.

21

SUPPER *and the* DAWNING *of a* NEW AGE

It has been another really busy day in the village. I bet everyone is really hungry. It's time for me to cook supper for my family now. At the party tonight, Grunter gave me a gift – something he says is very special...

This shiny new metal is called bronze, and Grunter told me he got it from a trader from another village. I wonder what people will use it for...

This could be the start of a new age... the Bronze Age!

GLOSSARY

butcher	to kill and cut up an animal for food
ceremonies	formal occasions celebrating achievements, people or religious events
crops	plants that are grown on a large scale because they are useful, usually as food
domesticated	animals that are tame and kept by humans
fertility	relating to the ability to produce offspring
herd	to gather large groups of animals in one place
hides	animal skins
mysterious	being unknown but interesting
nomads	people who do not live in one place
permanent	(intended to) last forever
surplus	to have more than is needed
technologies	inventions or methods based on scientific understanding or knowledge
temple	a place of worship
trade	to buy and sell goods

INDEX